DRAGONFLY BABIES

DAVID ROMANOSKY · DREW FALCHETTA

This is a dragonfly.

egg

This is a dragonfly egg.

eggs

The dragonfly mom has lots of eggs.

She puts the eggs in the water.

The dragonfly baby comes out.

Dragonfly babies live and eat in the water.

Dragonfly moms have wings. They can fly.

Dragonfly babies don't have wings. They swim.

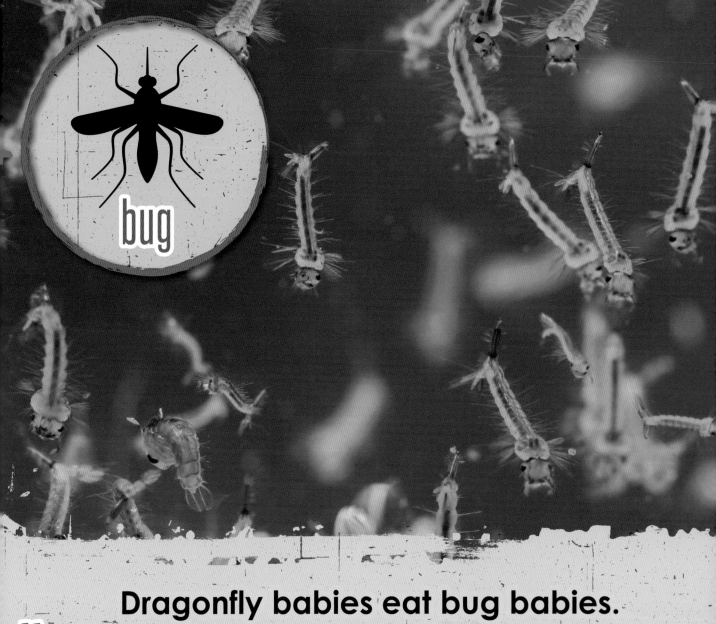

bug

Dragonfly babies eat bug babies.

Dragonfly babies eat frog babies.

The babies eat and eat and eat.

They get big.

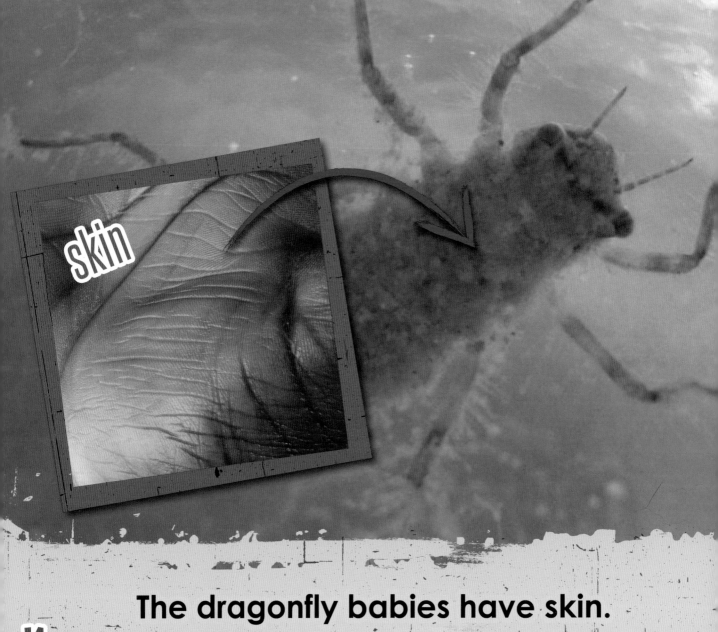

skin

The dragonfly babies have skin.

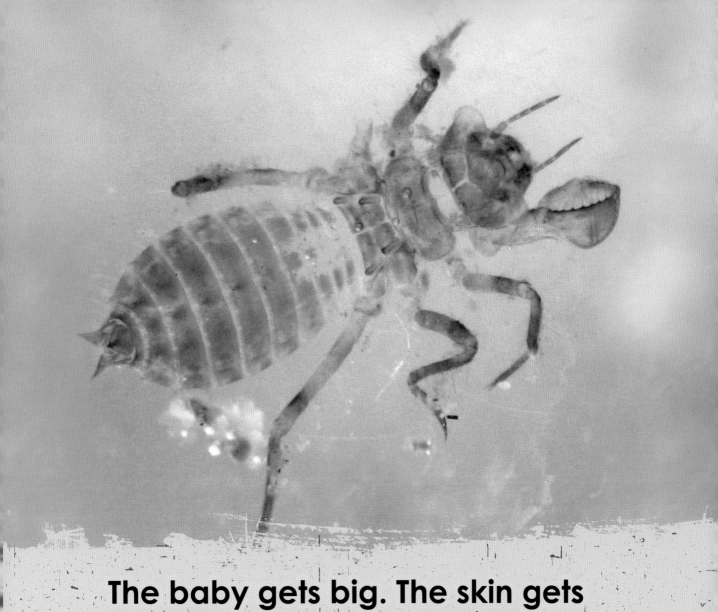

The baby gets big. The skin gets too little. The skin comes off.

There is new skin under it.

They get new big skin over
and over and over.

The dragonfly baby climbs out of the water.

The skin comes off.

Now he has four wings.

Now he is a dragonfly.

There he goes!

Up! Down! Across the sky!

DRAGONFLY BABY FACTS

A dragonfly egg takes about a week to hatch into a dragonfly larva, also called a nymph. A dragonfly nymph will molt between six and fifteen times before becoming an adult dragonfly.

Dragonfly nymphs live in the water until they are ready to become adult dragonflies. This stage can take up to five years.

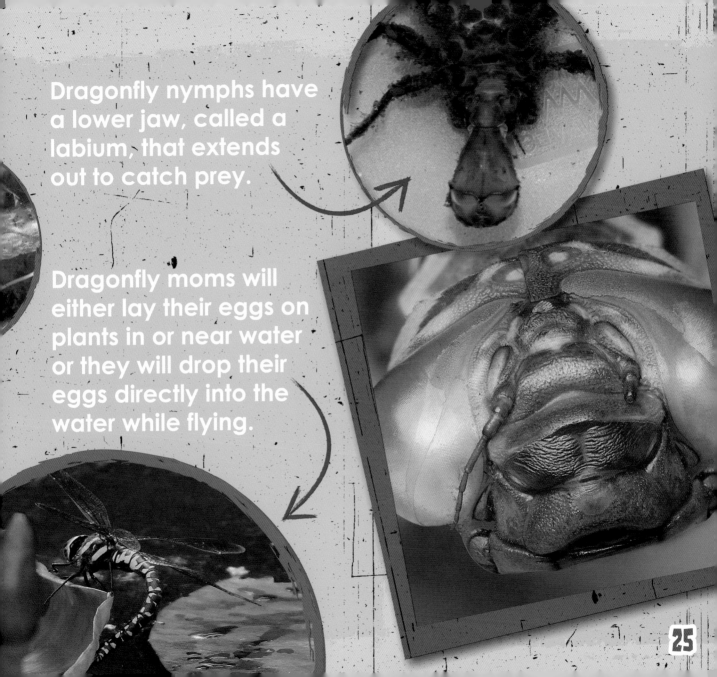

Dragonfly nymphs have a lower jaw, called a labium, that extends out to catch prey.

Dragonfly moms will either lay their eggs on plants in or near water or they will drop their eggs directly into the water while flying.

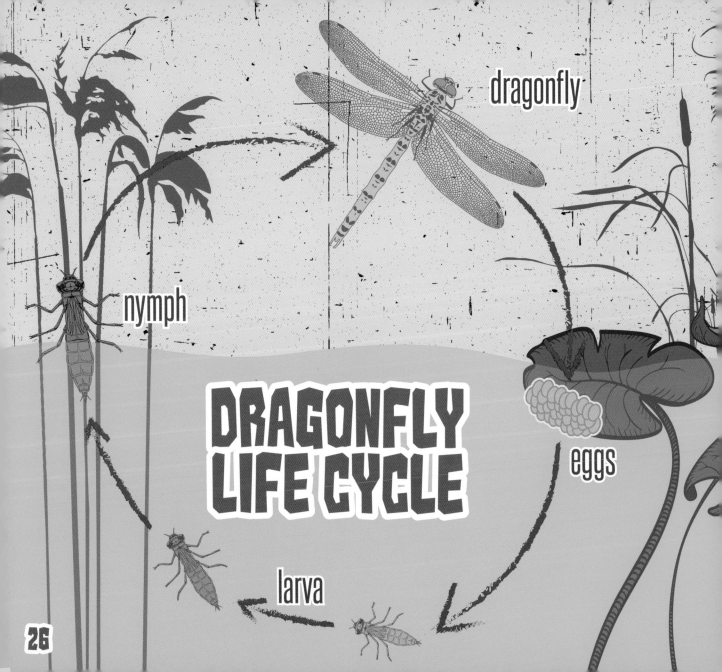

dragonfly

nymph

DRAGONFLY LIFE CYCLE

eggs

larva

I can match the words to the pictures using the first letter sounds.

dragonfly

frog

wing

baby

POWER WORDS

How many can you read?

across	don't	has	live	off	there
and	down	have	lots	out	they
baby	eat	he	mom	over	this
big	four	in	new	put	too
can	get	is	now	she	under
come	goes	little	of	the	up